The King Who Loved to Sing

by Spencer Brinker

Consultant:
Beth Gambro
Reading Specialist
Yorkville, Illinois

Contents

BEARPORT PUBLISHING

New York, New York

The King Who Loved to Sing

There once was a **king** who loved to **sing**.

He loved to **sing** in the fall and **spring**.

He loved to **sing** when he sat on a **swing**.

He loved to **sing**
with his arm in a **sling**.

He loved to **sing** and look at his blue **ring**.

If a bee gave him a **sting**, he still loved to **sing**.

The **king** really loved to **sing**.

It was his very favorite **thing**.

Key Words in the -ing Family

king **ring** **sing** **sling**

spring **sting** **swing**

Other **-ing** Words: **bring, string, wing**

Index

About the Author

Spencer Brinker loves to tell "dad jokes" and play word games with his twin girls.

Teaching Tips

Before Reading

✔ Introduce rhyming words and the **–ing** word family to readers.

✔ Guide readers on a "picture walk" through the text by asking them to name the things shown.

✔ Discuss book structure by showing children where text will appear consistently on pages. Highlight the supportive pattern of the book.

During Reading

✔ Encourage readers to "read with your finger" and point to each word as it is read. Stop periodically to ask children to point to a specific word in the text.

✔ Reading strategies: When encountering unknown words, prompt readers with encouraging cues such as:

- **Does that word look like a word you already know?**
- **Does it rhyme with another word you have already read?**

After Reading

✔ Write the key words on index cards.

- **Have readers match them to pictures in the book.**

✔ Ask readers to identify their favorite page in the book. Have them read that page aloud.

✔ Choose an **–ing** word. Ask children to pick a word that rhymes with it.

✔ Ask children to create their own rhymes using **–ing** words. Encourage them to use the same pattern found in the book.

Credits: Cover, © LifetimeStock/Shutterstock; 2–3, © LifetimeStock/Shutterstock and © Michael Drager/Shutterstock; 4, © LifetimeStock/Shutterstock and © Potapov Alexander/Shutterstock; 5, © LifetimeStock/Shutterstock, © yamix/Shutterstock, © jps/Shutterstock, and © byvalet/Shutterstock; 6–7, © LifetimeStock/Shutterstock and DnDavis/Shutterstock; 8–9, © LifetimeStock/Shutterstock and © Michael Drager/Shutterstock; 10–11, © LifetimeStock/Shutterstock; 12–13, © LifetimeStock/Shutterstock, irin-k/Shutterstock, and Seqoya/Shutterstock; 14–15, © LifetimeStock/Shutterstock; 16T (L to R), © LifetimeStock/Shutterstock, © LifetimeStock/Shutterstock and © Luba V Nel/Shutterstock, © LifetimeStock/Shutterstock, and © LifetimeStock/Shutterstock and © photomak/Shutterstock; 16B (L to R), © yamix/Shutterstock, © irin-k/Shutterstock, © karakedi35/Shutterstock, and © LifetimeStock/Shutterstock.

Publisher: Kenn Goin   **Senior Editor:** Joyce Tavolacci   **Creative Director:** Spencer Brinker

Library of Congress Cataloging-in-Publication Data: Names: Brinker, Spencer, author. | Gambro, Beth, consultant. Title: The king who loved to sing / by Spencer Brinker; consultant: Beth Gambro, Reading Specialist, Yorkville, Illinois. Description: New York, New York: Bearport Publishing, [2020] | Series: Read and rhyme: Level 3 | Includes index. Identifiers: LCCN 2019007171 (print) | LCCN 2019012633 (ebook) | ISBN 9781642806113 (Ebook) | ISBN 9781642805574 (library) | ISBN 9781642807264 (pbk.) Subjects: LCSH: Readers (Primary) | Singing—Juvenile fiction. Classification: LCC PE1119 (ebook) | LCC PE1119 .B751857 2020 (print) | DDC 428.6/2—dc23 LC record available at https://lccn.loc.gov/2019007171

10 9 8 7 6 5 4 3 2 1